b.┗.. ..⌐
Points: 1.0

UG

Explore the Outdoors

Hiking

Have Fun, Be Smart

by Sara Coppin

Published in 2000 by The Rosen Publishing Group, Inc.
29 East 21st Street, New York, NY 10010

First Edition

Library of Congress Cataloging-in-publication data

Coppin, Sara.
    Hiking : have fun, be smart / Sara Coppin.
      p. cm.— (Explore the outdoors)
    Includes bibliographical references and index.
    Summary: Discusses hiking as a teenage activity, discussing how to organize hikes, where to go, what kinds of equipment to use, and how to remain safe in the wild.
    ISBN 0-8239-3169-2 (lib. bdg.)
    1. Hiking—Juvenile literature. [1. Hiking.] I. Title. II. Series.

GV199.52 .C67 2000
796.51—dc21   99-047917

Manufactured in the United States of America

contents

Introduction

I went to the woods because I wished to live deliberately, to confront only the essential facts of life, and see if I could not learn what it had to teach, and not, when I came to die, discover that I had not lived.

Henry David Thoreau

Human beings have evolved a special skill: We can walk upright. By developing this upright, two-legged stance, humans freed their other two limbs for tasks such as being able to pick things up and carry them for long distances. What does this have to do with a book on hiking? Well, once we were able to walk upright, the major pastime of our species changed from climbing in and out of trees to taking off on foot, carrying our babies, tools, food and containers of water in our arms. And with that, humans became a species of hikers.

Webster's dictionary defines hiking as a "long walk, especially for pleasure or exercise," and says that this particular use of the word entered the English language in 1865. Of course, that's no reason to think that no one ever went on a long walk just for the fun of it until the 1800s. We can't really say that hundreds of thousands of years ago people didn't enjoy hiking. However, in the modern era, with its cars and

trains and airplanes, getting out on foot and taking a long walk is almost always a recreational choice. Today the reason for going on a hike isn't just to get from point A to point B. It's to get away from the stress of our daily lives; to take a break from cities, cement, and cars; to get closer to the natural world; and to enjoy getting exercise and spending time outside. We go hiking to have fun.

This book discusses many of the fun reasons why people take hikes today, from bird-watching to bonding with pals, from counting wildflowers to changing the way you think about life. There is lots of practical information in here, too, such as what to do when you see a bear, what to always have in your day pack, and how to make the most of your nearest wilderness areas. There are even some great

hiker biographies included so that you can learn about people who have been committed to enjoying the outdoors and preserving the natural world. Last but not least, you'll find tons of resources in the back of the book on recreational and environmental organizations, places to get your supplies, and Web sites, magazines, and books that you should check out before you head for the hills!

John Muir (1838–1914)
Explorer, Writer, and Conservationist

John Muir, one of America's most important conservationists, was born in Scotland, but emigrated with his family to Wisconsin when he was nine years old. At age twenty-nine, Muir left his job in Indianapolis and began his years of wandering the country. He walked one thousand miles from Indiana to the Gulf of Mexico, eventually ending up in California, where, though he would continue to travel the world, he made his home. The Sierra Nevada, and in particular the spectacular Yosemite valley, were the areas closest to Muir's heart. In 1874 he published the first of a series of articles entitled "Studies in the Sierra" that launched his career as a successful writer.

During his life-
time, he traveled
to Alaska,
Australia, South
America, Africa,
Europe, China,
and Japan, and
published 300
articles and ten

books on his travels and his naturalist
philosophy. He urged everyone to "climb the mountains
and get their good tidings." Often called the father of
our national park system, Muir helped to establish
Yosemite, Sequoia, Mount Rainier, Petrified Forest, and
Grand Canyon national parks, and in 1892 Muir founded
the Sierra Club, one of America's most influential conser-
vationist and environmental organizations, to "do something for wildness and make the mountains glad."

Thanks to the dedication of John Muir and the
Sierra Club, Americans have many protected wilderness
areas to explore and enjoy. Through his writings, he has
taught generations of people the importance of experi-
encing and preserving our natural heritage.

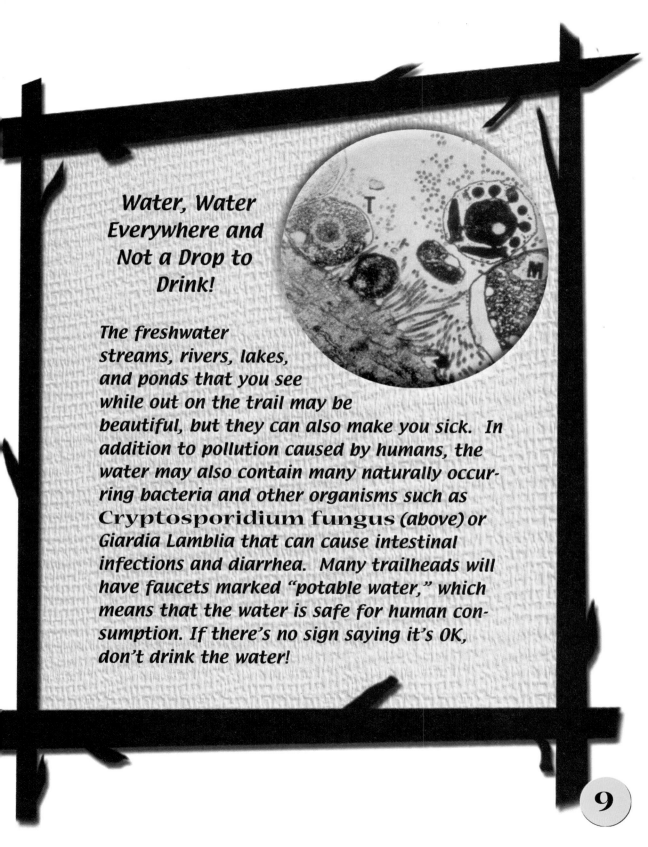

Water, Water Everywhere and Not a Drop to Drink!

The freshwater streams, rivers, lakes, and ponds that you see while out on the trail may be beautiful, but they can also make you sick. In addition to pollution caused by humans, the water may also contain many naturally occurring bacteria and other organisms such as Cryptosporidium fungus (above) or Giardia Lamblia that can cause intestinal infections and diarrhea. Many trailheads will have faucets marked "potable water," which means that the water is safe for human consumption. If there's no sign saying it's OK, don't drink the water!

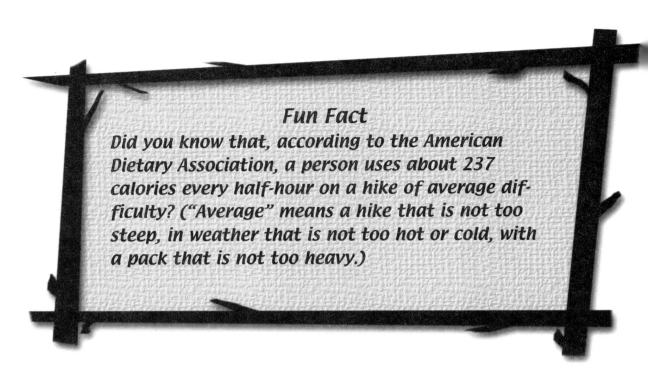

Fun Fact

Did you know that, according to the American Dietary Association, a person uses about 237 calories every half-hour on a hike of average difficulty? ("Average" means a hike that is not too steep, in weather that is not too hot or cold, with a pack that is not too heavy.)

1 Hiking Philosophies

Many cultures around the world are very involved with and respectful of their natural environments. Along with this respect there are often specific philosophies, or ways of thinking, about the relationship between humans and nature. Nature-focused religions, such as those of Native Americans, regard the earth and the plants and animals that live on it as equal to humans in their importance. People do not own the land, but belong to it, in a partnership with other living things. In many Native American religions, animals such as the crow and the coyote are believed to have great wisdom and lessons to teach to humans. Many different Native American cultures have rites of passage in which young people venture out alone into the wilderness, hiking far from camp and spending many nights in isolation to gain wisdom and courage from the experience.

The native people of Australia, known as Aborigines (the word "aborigine" means "from the beginning"), have a hiking tradition of their own that is also deeply rooted in a spiritual connection to the earth. The European colonists who settled in Australia coined the term "walkabout" to refer to the Aborigines' roaming way of life. To the Europeans, who believed in having fixed, permanent homes, the partly nomadic lifestyle of the native Australians seemed to stem from a compulsive, or

uncontrollable, urge to travel about the land. The truth is that the Australian Aborigines have very complex religious and practical ties to the landscape and have connections to many different sites spread across the land for hundreds of miles. An individual may spend his or her life "on walkabout," traveling to various sites of spiritual importance and making a living from the land along the way.

Outdoor Sports and Environmental Organizations

Getting outdoors and into nature, whether it's a wilderness area far from civilization or a recreation area just outside of town, can be an uplifting experience. Sometimes it can be a challenge, though. For those who live in big cities, it may be difficult to get out of the urban environment. Anyone without a driver's license and a car may find transportation unavailable or inaccessible. It may be hard for young people to organize a group that includes adult supervision. Because their founders believed that hiking and enjoying and protecting the natural world were important things to do, organizations such as the Boy Scouts and Girl Scouts of America and Outward Bound help kids all over the country to participate

in outdoor activities in natural environments. These organizations don't just help young people take a trip to the country. They also teach them important things about cooperation, community, and facing challenges.

The two best American scouting organizations are the Boy Scouts of America and the Girl Scouts of America. There are many other scouting groups around the country, including other national organizations such as Campfire Boys and Girls, as well as smaller local organizations you may find in your area. Check the Resources section in the back of this book for more information.

Most scouting groups have a similar mission and work in similar ways. Their basic philosophy is that there are important things young people can learn by spending time in the wilderness that they wouldn't be able to learn in a classroom. Scout troops are clubs for boys and girls that teach a variety of different activities, but they place a special emphasis on the outdoors and community service. If you live in a city or suburb and you are a member of a scouting club, you may not go hiking every day, but you will probably participate in a few camping trips throughout the year. You will learn things about camping and hiking safety from your scout leader, and you will have his or her help in organizing trips. You will make friends with other scouts in your troop and have people your age with whom to share outdoor adventures. In addition, you will participate in projects designed to help your community. Depending on where you live, these projects could be anything from reading to the elderly or cleaning up city lots and making gardens to starting recycling programs. Often it is up to the scouts themselves to decide on what kinds of projects their troop will work.

Outward Bound is another outdoors organization

designed especially for young people. Unlike the scouting groups, Outward Bound is not a club. It's more like a wilderness school. The idea of a school may not sound like much fun, but this is a different kind of learning experience. The hiking philosophy of the Outward Bound organization can be summed up by their five core values: adventure and challenge; compassion and service; learning through experience; personal development; and social and environmental responsibility.

On an Outward Bound course, groups of six to twelve people (that's four to ten students plus one instructor and one assistant) are in the wilderness for a certain number of days. By facing outdoor challenges as a team, students learn about themselves as well as how to reach out and help other members of the team. In addition to these lessons, Outward Bound courses teach cutting-edge techniques on backcountry survival, including the environmental philosophy and practice of Leave No Trace camping and travel. This practice involves living a simple, self-reliant, low-impact lifestyle in the wilderness. The goal is to reap the rewards and benefits of nature while at the same time leaving behind no evidence that you have been there.

In addition to Outward Bound, there are many local organizations such as the Youth Enrichment Services Outdoor Adventure Program in New England, and Seattle Inner-City Outings in Washington State. These groups help youths from urban areas who would not otherwise be able to take trips to wilderness areas. Their philosophy is that no matter where you live or how much money you have, you should be able to enjoy the richness and tranquility of the outdoors.

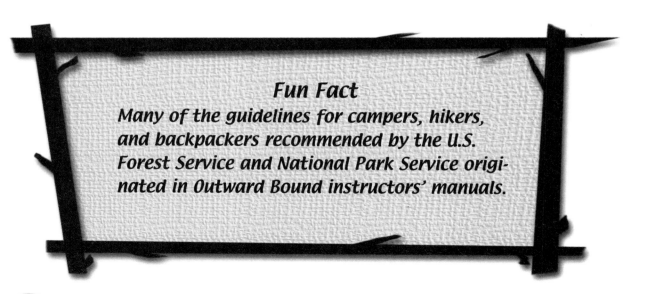

Fun Fact
Many of the guidelines for campers, hikers, and backpackers recommended by the U.S. Forest Service and National Park Service originated in Outward Bound instructors' manuals.

Juliette Gordon Low (1860–1927), Founder of the Girl Scouts of America

Born to a wealthy family in Savannah, Georgia, Juliette, or "Daisy" as she was called, was in her fifties when she began the work for which she is remembered. In 1912, she dreamed of starting something in America that would be "for all the girls." She envisioned an organization that would help bring girls out of their sheltered and stifling home environments into the world, to experience the outdoors and serve in their communities. Before women had even won the right to vote in the United States, Daisy founded the Girl Scouts of America, and soon groups of young girls were hiking through the woods, playing basketball, going camping together, and learning first-aid and outdoor cooking techniques—all activities that were seen as foolish and improper for girls during that time.

Today the Girl Scouts continue Juliette Gordon Low's mission with programs such as Eco-Action, a nationwide environmental program, and various national health and fitness and sports projects for girls and young women across the country.

2 Packing It In

Let's get right to the point. Here is a checklist of things that you should always have in your day pack, and some short explanations as to why. Let's begin with the pack itself.

A Comfortable Pack

Your pack doesn't have to be huge, just big enough for one day's worth of trail supplies. It should be sturdy, comfortable, and easy to put on. A regular school backpack is fine. (Just be sure to take your textbooks out!)

Water

The most important thing to have with you is plenty of water. Bring water from home in used spring water or juice bottles. If you're hiking in hot weather, bring about 32 ounces of water for every two hours you are on the trail. To have cold water at midday, try freezing a few bottles the night before. As the ice melts in the hot sun, you'll have cool water to drink.

Wristwatch

Other than water, a wristwatch is probably the second most important thing to bring on your hike. Unless you can tell accurate time by the sun (and we're NOT daring you to try), having a watch is an essential way for you to track your progress along the trail and make sure that you get back to base on time.

A Small Flashlight

Hopefully you won't need this, but if for some reason the sun does set while you are still out on the trail, you will need to find your way out. A small but reliable flashlight will not take up much space in your pack and will give you a nice feeling of security. (Make sure you have fresh batteries.)

Matches or a Lighter in a Waterproof Container

As with the flashlight, you hope that you will never need these, but you don't want to need them and not have them.

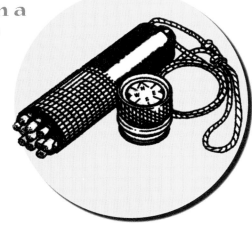

Pocketknife

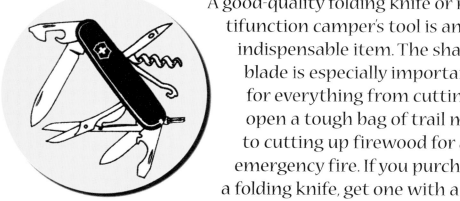

A good-quality folding knife or multifunction camper's tool is an indispensable item. The sharp blade is especially important for everything from cutting open a tough bag of trail mix to cutting up firewood for an emergency fire. If you purchase a folding knife, get one with a lock blade that won't accidentally close on your fingers.

Money (Credit Cards, Coins, and Cash)

Money? No, it's not to buy dirt from the squirrels. Should you lose your way along the trail and end up on a road you don't recognize and need to use a pay phone, or if you pass by a remote mountain lodge that serves apple pie and ice cream, money is important, even in the middle of nowhere. Besides, you wouldn't want to leave all your money in your car at the trailhead and have it stolen from the car.

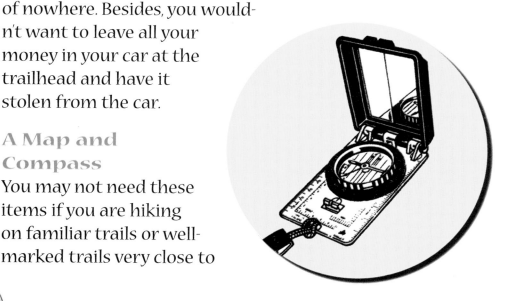

A Map and Compass

You may not need these items if you are hiking on familiar trails or well-marked trails very close to civilization, but if you are planning to hike into remote areas, you would be foolish to go in "blind."

Sunscreen
This item is a must for any outdoor activity.

Insect Repellent
In spray-on or lotion form, this item is a lifesaver during spring and summer, when mosquitoes are out in hungry abundance.

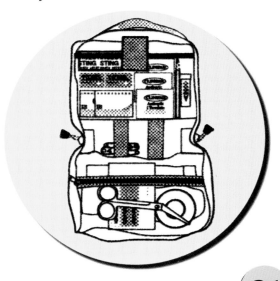

Snacks
Bringing a little food is important for any hike, particularly if you plan to be out for more than four or five hours. Hiking burns a lot of calories, and at least some of those calories must be replaced. The alternative is early exhaustion and lethargy. Simple, healthy foods such as raisins and peanuts, baked tofu, apples, cheese, jerky, and energy bars are all good hiking fare.

A First-Aid Kit
Small camper's or traveler's first-aid kits are available and can be very useful for minor injuries such as cuts, splinters, burns, and rashes. However,

unless you are planning on hiking into a fairly remote area, they are not absolutely necessary. If you want to put your own kit together, include the following items: bandages, gauze, Band-Aids, tweezers, aspirin, antihistamine (for allergic reactions), and baking soda (which can be made into a paste and used to soothe burns and bug bites).

Clean, Dry Socks

Wet socks can ruin your whole day, causing blisters and chills.

Bandanna

This multipurpose item hardly weighs a thing, and you can use it as a handkerchief, washcloth, towel, sweatband, pot holder, or compress.

Dental Floss

Another tiny item with many uses, including clothesline, replacement shoelace, sewing thread, and fishing line.

Cellular Phone

This is an optional item, but it is something that, if you already own one, is a good thing to bring with you. Wireless phones may not work in the wilderness area where you will be hiking, so find out first if the range of your phone is adequate. We recommend turning off the phone while you hike. This will save the batteries and free you from the "pollution" of the modern world. You're trying to get away from it all, anyway, aren't you? Only use the phone in an emergency.

Trail Tip

Sore feet make hiking a pain—literally! Try the following tricks to help unhappy feet:

- Feet and ankles start to swell in the middle of the day from heat as well as use. To cope with swollen feet and avoid the blisters that are caused by tight boots, start the day wearing two pairs of socks and take off one set when you stop for lunch. Your feet will feel freer and your shoes looser.

- Take a break mid-hike and give your hot and tired feet a cooling rub with rubbing alcohol.

- Carry a little "foot kit" that includes the following items: moleskin, second skin or liquid bandage, rubbing alcohol, and toenail clippers.

3 What's a Hike Like?

If you think that hiking just means putting on big boots, grabbing your walking stick, and heading up the side of a mountain to do a little afternoon yodeling, think again! The types of hikes you can go on are as varied as the natural environments that exist around the world. From jungles to deserts, from glaciers to coastlines, Mother Nature offers an amazing

Hiking on loose ground, particularly when that loose ground is found on hillsides and slopes, is going to be more of a workout than the rolling hills hike. It will also take more concentration and physical effort to maintain your footing. Higher altitudes have thin air, which means that there is less oxygen in the air you are breathing than at lower altitudes. You may not notice it at first, but after some exercise, you may be more tired and shorter of breath than you expected. The distance you feel comfortable covering in a certain period of time will likely be shorter than on a less rigorous hike, so be careful not to get into a situation where you over-extend yourself.

River Gorges

River gorges are the canyons that rivers cut through the landscape. They may or may not have a river running through them year-round, since water levels can fluctuate dramatically from season to season.

     The terrain of a river gorge, like the skree mountainside, is usually made up of loose, unstable rocks and can be quite steep in places. But river gorges also have giant boulders that are smooth and rounded and usually very stable and fun to climb on. The best time of year to hike in a river gorge is in high, hot summer. Why? Well, as long as the river itself is calm and the current is slow, with a pair of sturdy hiking sandals (old sneakers will do as well), a bathing suit, T-shirt, and plenty of sunscreen, you could make your hike part walk, part swim! Hike upstream alongside the river, and when you've gone sufficiently far and you're getting hot and dusty and ready for a swim, carefully climb down to the water level and get in the river. Keep your sandals on and sit back in the water with your feet pointed downstream. This will allow you to feel your way with protected feet and to steer with your legs. Then let the gentle current of the river carry you slowly

back downstream to where you started. You'll finish your hot, dusty hike feeling cool and refreshed!

Please note that it is not safe to swim in rivers with white water, or in rivers that are very deep or wide, and it's NEVER safe to swim alone. Even a seemingly calm river can be rough and dangerous in certain parts, so keep an eye out for risky areas as you hike along the river, and pay attention once you are in the water. If you begin to feel the current pulling you enough to make it difficult for you to control your movements, calmly swim with the current back to solid ground and get out and walk. Try to avoid swimming against the current, as you will quickly become exhausted and will be more easily overwhelmed by the current. Be careful, and be smart!

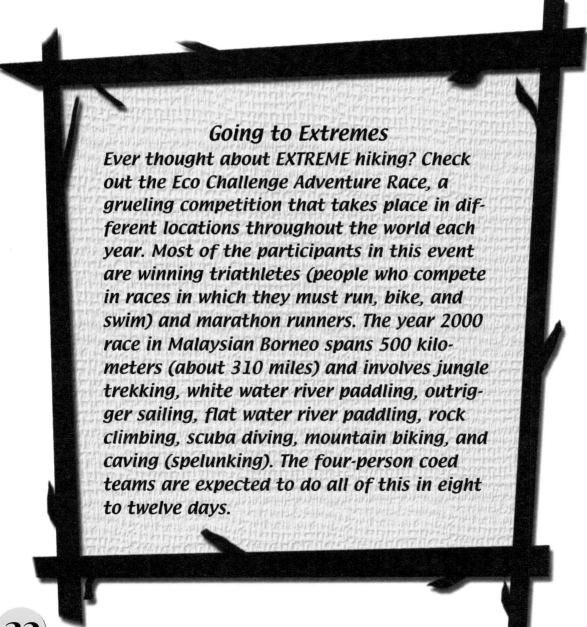

Going to Extremes

Ever thought about EXTREME hiking? Check out the Eco Challenge Adventure Race, a grueling competition that takes place in different locations throughout the world each year. Most of the participants in this event are winning triathletes (people who compete in races in which they must run, bike, and swim) and marathon runners. The year 2000 race in Malaysian Borneo spans 500 kilometers (about 310 miles) and involves jungle trekking, white water river paddling, outrigger sailing, flat water river paddling, rock climbing, scuba diving, mountain biking, and caving (spelunking). The four-person coed teams are expected to do all of this in eight to twelve days.

Steep, Hard Ground

Most trails make steep uphill climbs easier by switchbacking, or zigzagging, gradually up the mountainside. Switchbacks make a trail longer in distance (since the shortest distance between the start of a trail and the top of a mountain is a straight line, and a switchback trail is a crazy, crooked path) but the steepness of the climb is not as dramatic. Of course, switchbacks or no, an uphill trail is a serious workout. You may quickly get hot and sweaty and tired. Don't feel bad if you need to stop and rest for a minute before continuing. Be sure to drink plenty of that water you're carrying. Your shoes should be lightweight and provide good traction. Tired legs appreciate good ankle support, so check out a pair of lightweight hiking boots. When choosing clothing, think layers. You want to be able to strip down to the minimum amount of clothing as you get hot and sweaty puffing up that hill. But don't forget to tie a sweatshirt around your waist. You'll need it later.

One important rule of hiking is that if you go up, you've also got to come down. It may seem tiring to hike uphill, but hiking back down a steep hill is also very strenuous and can be really hard on your feet and knees. Gravity can work against you as your tired feet pound against hard ground. Your toes may jam into the tips of your shoes, and the balls of your feet may chafe against your insoles. The last leg of your hike can be unpleasant if you're not prepared for this terrain.

Sturdy, supportive shoes or boots are best for steep hiking. Sneakers that may have seemed comfortable on the way

Trail Tip
When encountering steep downhill terrain, try making your own little switchbacks along the trail by walking with your feet pointed to one side or the other and not straight down the mountain. Walk to the left for a few steps and then turn to the right and walk that way, making gradual progress down the hill as you go. This will save your toes and help you keep your balance on the steep slope!

up might not be sturdy enough or provide sufficient traction on the way down the mountain. Try not to attempt terrain like this in shoes that have not yet been broken in.

You may find that you begin to get a little chilly as you start heading downhill. Your muscles produce more heat during the aerobic exercise of carrying your weight up the mountain. Even though you may be moving faster on the way down, you are not getting the same workout. The sweat from the uphill climb may start to chill you a little. This is the time to put on the sweatshirt that you have tied around your waist. And you thought you would never need it!

Climate

The climate of a particular area is the average course or condition of weather, including temperature, precipitation, and wind, over a certain period of time. Climates may change with the seasons, but they are predictable enough for you to prepare for your hike. You should not try to hike in extreme weather conditions (snowy or below-zero weather, extremely high altitudes, or arid, dry landscapes with little water or shelter) unless you are very experienced and outfitted with specialized outdoor survival gear.

The most likely hazardous climatic conditions you will face on your hikes will be low temperatures. Water freezes at 32 degrees Fahrenheit, and you should not hike out into the wilderness in freezing conditions. You should not camp in an area with nighttime temperatures below freezing unless you are experienced and well equipped. Avoid rain, fog, and dry heat as well.

Hypothermia is a serious, and even deadly, condition that people can develop if exposed to cold temperatures. It happens when the body temperature dips below 95 degrees Fahrenheit (normal body temperature is 98.6 degrees). Every year people die of exposure to the elements, many of them on simple day hikes in 40-degree to 50-degree weather. To prevent hypothermia, dress in layered clothing. Adjust your layers as often as necessary to stay comfortable throughout your hike. Never let yourself become chilled or too soaked with perspiration. If temperatures are dropping, be sure to monitor yourself and your companions for the signs of hypothermia: chills, shivering, lethargy, lack of coordination, and irrational behavior.

If you notice these symptoms, stop and seek shelter. Remove the wet clothing and put on all of the dry clothing available. Cover the head and neck, as these are the areas where the body loses more than half of its heat. Huddle together to generate body heat. Build a fire and drink hot liquids.

Preparing for rainy or foggy conditions on a hike is crucial. Find out what the rain patterns are for the area in which you plan to hike. What have the current weather conditions been like? Weather is not totally predictable, of course, but you can get enough of an idea of what to expect to avoid danger. Pack lightweight rain gear in case of surprise showers or thick fog (both of which can soak your clothes and put you at risk for hypothermia). Wear a wide-brimmed hat to keep your head dry and to keep water out of your eyes. Pack lots of snacks and, even if you do not plan to camp, always bring matches in a waterproof container.

Extremely hot conditions can be dangerous, too, mostly because of the risks of dehydration and heatstroke. The average active adult needs to drink three to six quarts of water per day. Hiking in desert conditions can require three gallons per day! And don't forget that in a climate like that, the only water you can count on having is the water you carry. Signs of dehydration and heatstroke include: no need to urinate; lack of perspiration; hot, dry skin; labored breathing; dizziness; nausea; and stomach or muscle cramps. If you notice symptoms of

Trail Tip

Your body doesn't just lose water when you sweat. You also lose electrolytes, which are essential components of your blood. Sports drinks such as Gatorade or Powerade have electrolytes in them, but in a pinch you can put together your own rehydrating drink. Linda Frederick Yaffe, author of The Well-Organized Camper, suggests this recipe:

7.5 ounces of cool water
1 tablespoon of sugar
1 tablespoon of fruit juice or powdered
    fruit juice mix
pinch of salt

dehydration in yourself or others, get out of the sun and into the shade, rest, drink water, and if possible, bathe the skin in cool water (but don't just jump in, as that can cause shock).

Camping

For many people, camping and hiking go hand in hand. There are many kinds of camping, including car or RV camping and backpacking. Backpacking means carrying all of the necessary supplies on your back and hiking into the wilderness to spend one or more nights.

If you plan to camp, you should find out what the camping rules are for the area in which you will be staying. National parks have strict rules about where and what time of year backpackers can camp and build campfires, and many campgrounds require that you make reservations for a site. The rules are established for the safety of the visitors of the park area and should not be taken lightly. One reason for these seasonal restrictions has to do with the risk of wildfires. In many wilderness areas, high summer (usually from late July through September) means dry grass and leaves. Deliberate arson, camper accidents, and even naturally occurring lightning can start deadly wildfires that can trap park visitors. In certain areas, there may be seasonal dangers caused by wildlife. We've all heard about the dangers of getting too close to a mother bear and her cubs! Camping reservations are a way for rangers to keep track of the number of people staying in the park at a

Trail Tip

In many national parks, campfires have been outlawed because of their destructive impact on the natural landscape. If you're hiking in an area where campfires are now illegal and you see an old fire ring or site, dismantle it.

- Disperse the rocks from the fire area to more natural-looking spots, placing the burned side down.
- Pick up any litter and carry it out with you.
- Break up or cover the burned ground with dirt or gravel.

given time. This information can help them to determine if and where a park visitor has gone missing. Both national parks and private campgrounds charge nightly fees.

Once you know the rules of the area where you plan to backpack and camp, the next step is to get a map of the area and to collect the necessary supplies for an overnight adventure. In addition to the items listed in chapter three, here are the basic camping necessities:

Backpack

A large pack, usually designed with a semiflexible frame to help the pack keep its shape when full, is a good choice. Make sure that the pack is comfortable to carry even when heavy by trying it on with weights in it BEFORE heading out on the trail.

Tent

Backpacking tents are incredibly light and fairly easy to assemble, but always make sure that you have assembled your particular tent once or twice BEFORE you go camping.

Ground Cloth

This plastic sheet goes on the ground before the tent is put up and protects the bottom of the tent from punctures, rain, snow, and dirt. Many tents have a sewn-in ground cloth.

Sleeping Bag

This should be a lightweight and easily compacted bag with either synthetic or down fill.

Sleeping Pad

This pad need only be as long as your torso to provide enough padding for you to sleep comfortably on hard ground.

Personal Medications

You should pack a supply of any medications that you take regularly, including directions for use.

Water Filter or Iodine Tablets

Unless you plan to boil all your water for three minutes, you should be equipped to treat water. You will not be able to pack enough water for more than one day of hiking.

Camping Pots, Spoons, Cups

You can buy kits that will have everything you need in a compact, easy-to-pack form. Don't worry about forks; you'll be fine with spoons and your pocketknife.

Backpacker Stove and Fuel

Small, single-burner stoves powered by small natural gas canisters are the easiest and most reliable.

Cleaning Supplies

Bring biodegradable soap, salt (useful as a gargle and a cleanser as well as a food seasoning), and a sponge.

Food

Bring food that is lightweight, not easily spoilable, and easy to prepare, such as dehydrated fruits and vegetables, instant oatmeal, hot cocoa, tea, flat breads, pasta, couscous, dried meats, and hard cheeses. Meal replacement or supplement bars are good as snacks but not enough to live on when backpacking.

Please be aware that there are many more items that are necessary for camping, depending on the climate of the area in which you are camping, the number of days you plan to be out, the distance you will be from civilization, how many people you will be camping with, and a great many other factors. When planning a camping trip, be sure to gather information and advice from a variety of sources and always go with at least one person who has a fair amount of camping experience.

4 Trail Safety

This is a strange and beautiful world, and it could be said that danger lurks around every corner. Safety is a concern whether you are on a city street, the parking lot of a suburban supermarket, or out on a wilderness trail. We cannot hide from the world for fear of danger, because we will miss out on the beauty. The only thing we can do is to keep our wits about us and prepare as best we can.

When planning a hike or thinking about spending time outdoors, safety is always something that should be in the back of your mind. If you plan ahead and educate yourself as much as you can, you will enjoy much more your outdoor recreation. Throughout this book we have listed safety tips for hiking, such as how to avoid hypothermia and dehydration, what to carry in your pack in case of emergencies, how to avoid getting stranded in the woods, and other ideas. In this chapter, we will go over a few other dangers you may encounter on wilderness hikes. Once again, remember that when planning a hike, you should become familiar with the specific area in which you are hiking, so that you can prepare for the particular risks involved.

Above all, the most important safety precaution to take when going hiking is never to go on a long hike alone. We cannot stress that enough. Many experienced hikers do enjoy being for ticks, focusing on your groin area, behind your knees, on your neck, and in your armpits. Check frequently when hiking in dense vegetation and try using insect repellent on your clothes to discourage hitchhiking ticks from sticking around.

If you are bitten by a tick, remove the entire tick by using rubbing alcohol or petroleum jelly to smother it. This will either kill the tick or cause it to let go and back out. If you remove the tick, but the head remains embedded in your skin, go to the doctor.

Lightning
If you get caught in an electrical storm, take cover. Get off peaks and ridges. You want to keep a low profile, so stay out of clearings, but also stay away from the tallest trees. From a sheltered place, relax and enjoy the light show!

Poison Ivy, Poison Oak, and Sumac
These plants produce resins on their leaves and branches that cause itchy rashes and, depending on how severely allergic you are, seriously debilitating reactions. Learn which of these plants you are most likely to encounter on your hike and how to identify them. If you think you may have touched one, try not

to spread the resin around. Avoid touching your face and other parts of your body with hands that have touched the exposed area. Wash the area with water, but do not use soap, which helps to spread it. If you can, change out of the clothing you suspect might have touched the plant.

If you develop a reaction, which appears as a red, bumpy, spreading rash, use calamine lotion to soothe the itching. An antihistamine, which helps to block the body's allergic reactions, also may be helpful.

Getting Lost

We've already said a few words about how to avoid getting lost, but there are additional steps you can take to make sure that this doesn't happen, and that if it does, you are able to relocate either your home base or the rest of your group.

First of all, carry a map and compass when going deep into wilderness areas. Most of the time you will use a topographical, or "topo," map for such areas, which shows natural landmarks such as hills, peaks, valleys, and bodies of water where there are no roads to reference. These maps work differently from the way street maps do, so be sure you know how to read a topo map before you head out. If you have a compass, be sure you know how to read it and that you know which direction you'll need to head in to get back to home base. Don't forget that a compass is only useful if you already have your orientation. You have to know where you are to get to where you want to go. The rule is, always know where you are, in what direction you have been hiking, and for how long. Locating yourself from a completely unknown position, even with map and compass, is not easy. Landmarks on the map may not be visible on the ground, or may look quite different from what you expect.

If you are hiking with a group, be sure to establish a meeting place along the trail (or you can agree to meet at home base) if you become separated. Make sure that everyone in the group is very clear about the plan. Another useful thing to have in case you become separated from your hiking companions is a whistle. The shrill sound is distinctive and will carry for some distance. Only blow the whistle in emergencies. One blast of the whistle every thirty seconds or so will help your party to locate you. Three blasts in a row is the universal call for help.

Trail Tip

- While hiking, pay constant attention to landmarks along the trail. Make mental and even written notes of features and the order in which you see them as you hike, so that if you need to turn and go back, you can recognize where you are and have a ballpark idea of how far you need to go.
- Be suspicious if a very clear trail suddenly becomes very faint; you may have taken a wrong turn without realizing it.
- Always remain calm if you become lost. Stop walking until you reorient yourself.

5 Fun Hiking Ideas

Hiking is great exercise and a great way to get away from the stress of everyday life, but it is not just about walking. There are a bunch of different fun activities you can incorporate into your hike. Here are just a few suggestions.

Identifying Birds, Animals, and Plants

Pick up a book at your local library or bookstore about the plants and animals of the area where you will be hiking. Many different guidebooks are available that are small enough to carry easily in

your backpack and that are full of beautiful color illustrations and photos that can help you to identify wildflowers, trees, other native plants, birds, mammals, reptiles, and even insects. Your natural heritage will be so much more precious to you when you take notice of all the diversity of the life around you. So many different plants and creatures call the wilderness their home, it is important that we preserve and appreciate it.

Trail Tip
Go on a wildflower walk! In the spring, take your wildflower guidebook out with you and try to count the number of different species of wildflowers you can spot. You will be amazed by how many different kinds of flowers there are in your area that you have never even noticed before!

Study the History of the Area
Many national parks and trails have important and fascinating roles in the history of this country. Just by doing a little research at the library or even on-line, you can discover amazing things about an area. Maybe the region of your hike was once the home of Native Americans who left things such as arrowheads, paintings, or carvings on stone, mortar holes in

The Wilderness and Struggling Teens

Unlike your parents, unlike your teachers, principals, and guidance counselors, unlike social workers and judges and all of the other authority figures you may meet in your life, Mother Nature is inflexible and unforgiving. She accepts no excuses and punishes swiftly and harshly all mistakes of judgment. Survival in the wilderness requires good judgment, maturity, a sense of responsibility, discipline, patience, and an appreciation for the consequences of one's acts.

For this reason, many wilderness leaders and educators believe that wilderness programs offer an excellent learning experience for troubled teens. Young people who have behavioral problems, who lack self-esteem, or who have been in trouble with the law all seem to derive enormous benefit from an outdoor experience. For more information about wilderness programs aimed at troubled children, visit the Web site Places for Struggling Teens at http://www.strugglingteens.com/therapy.html.

the bedrock, or other physical evidence of their lives. Find out more. Who were these people? How did they live? When and why did they move from this place? Are there any remaining members of the tribe living nearby?

You may be hiking on an old immigrant trail used by settlers from the East seeking new lives in the West. Where were they from? When did this happen? What was the cross-country journey like? Where did they eventually settle? You could be hiking trails used by Native Americans, trappers, missionaries, conquistadors, naturalists, stagecoaches, miners, lumberjacks, and outlaws. Explore the history of your wilderness areas. You may even learn something about your own family's history in the process!

Henry David Thoreau (1817–1862), Writer, Naturalist

Henry David Thoreau is one of the most influential writers of American literature. His essay on civil disobedience influenced great leaders such as Gandhi and Martin Luther King Jr. In 1845, Thoreau moved from the town of Concord, Massachusetts, to the remote area of Walden Pond. During his years there, he wrote many works that contributed to the literary and philosophical movement known as American transcendentalism. He also carefully recorded the natural history of the area. Because of his love of the outdoors and his great appreciation of the wilderness, he is sometimes called the father of the American conservation and preservation movements. In his essay entitled "Walking," Thoreau writes: "I think I cannot preserve my health and spirits, unless I spend four hours a day—and it is commonly more than that—sauntering through the woods and over the hills and fields, absolutely free from all worldly engagements."

Learn About Yourself

You can learn a lot about yourself by spending time in the wilderness. Sometimes the trappings of our lives and the details of our daily routines get in the way of who we really are. When you're planning your hike with your companions, you may want to agree ahead of time to make a stop along the way where each of you can take a little time out from the group. Go sit on a rock on your own, a little distance from the others. You may find that, in quiet moments, you begin to forget about the worries that plague you. You gain a new perspective on things. Try bringing your journal or diary with you. If you don't already have one, this may be a good time to start keeping one.

You may also consider bringing a sketchbook or watercolor set with you. You may find great inspiration in the solitude. Bring a camera. Express your thoughts and your feelings creatively. Close your eyes for a moment and listen to the sounds of nature around you. Take a deep breath and smell the freshness and fullness of the air. Then open your eyes again. Try looking at things in a new way.

Glossary

Altitude
The height, or vertical elevation, above a surface, usually measured in feet or meters (approximately three feet) above sea level.

Bacteria
Single-celled microrganisms. Some are beneficial to human beings, and some cause a variety of diseases.

Climate
The general pattern of weather for a particular geographical area as measured over a certain length of time, such as a season, a year, or longer.

Conservationist
A person who believes in preserving the natural environment.

Dehydration
A severe loss of bodily fluids, which can be fatal.

Electrolytes
Essential chemical elements found in bodily fluids.

Hypothermia
A dangerous, potentially fatal reduction in body temperature caused by exposure to the cold.

Leave No Trace
The modern, environmentally conscious hiker's credo, which means that you should not disturb the wilderness by leaving rubbish behind you. Another expression is "Take nothing but pictures; leave nothing but footprints."

Potable
Safe for drinking.

Species
A class or group of living organisms having certain common features and being capable of reproducing .

Terrain
The physical features of an area of land.

Topographical
The representation of geographical features in graphic (drawn or printed) form, such as a topographical map.

Trailhead
The point at which a trail begins.

Resources

Where to Learn More About Hiking

Inner City Outings (ICO)
The Sierra Club Foundation/ICO
85 Second Street, 2nd Floor
San Francisco, CA 94105
(415) 977-5628
e-mail: national.outings@sierraclub.org
Web site: http://www.sierraclub.org/outings/ico

Outward Bound USA
100 Mystery Point Road
Garrison, NY 10524
(888) 88-BOUND
Web site: http://www.outwardbound.com

Youth Challenge Program
Temagami Wilderness Centre Limited
Suite 210, 3600 Billings Court
Burlington, Ontario L7N 3N6
(905) 632-8123
e-mail: info@temagami.com
Web site: http://www.temagami.com

Youth Enrichment Services
412 Massachusetts Avenue
Boston, MA 02118
(617) 267-5877
Web site: http://www.yeskids.org

Web Sites

Eco Challenge
http://www.ecochallenge.com

Girl Scouts of America
http://www.girlscouts.net

Great Recreation Pages
http://www.gorp.com

Outside Online
http://outsidemag.com

Pacific Crest Trail Association
http://www.pcta.org

Sierra Club
http://www.sierraclub.org/

For Further Reading

George, Jean Craighead. *My Side of the Mountain.* New York: Puffin Books, 1975.

Griggs, Jack L. *All the Birds of North America: American Bird Conservancy's Field Guide.* New York: HarperCollins, 1997.

Harmon, Will. *Wild Country Companion.* Helena, MT: Falcon Press Publishing, 1994.

Mowat, Farley. *Never Cry Wolf.* New York: Bantam Books, 1983.

Ross, Cindy and Todd Gladfelter. *Kids in the Wild.* Seattle, WA: The Mountaineers, 1995.

Thoreau, Henry David. *Walden.* New York: St. Martin's Press, 2000.

Yaffe, Linda. *The Well-Organized Camper.* Chicago, IL: Chicago Review Press, 1999.

Zim, Herbert Spencer, and Alexander C. Martin. *Trees: A Guide to Familiar American Trees.* New York: Golden Books Publishing Company, 1987.

Index

Credits

About the Author

Sara Coppin grew up in northern California, where she hiked in the Sierra Nevada mountains, read banned books, and listened to punk music because there wasn't much else to do.

Photo Credits

Cover photo © Cheyenne Rouse/Mountain Stock; p. 5 © Dan Blackburn/Mountain Stock; pp. 6, 33, 52 © Cheyenne Rouse/Mountain Stock; p. 8 © CORBIS;p. 9 © CORBIS/Lester V. Bergman; p. 12 © SuperStock; p. 13 © CORBIS/Kevin T. Gilbert; p. 15 © CORBIS; p.24 © CORBIS/ Neil Rabinowitz; p. 25 © Rob Gage/FPG; pp. 27, 31 © Larry Carver/ Mountain Stock; p.29 © Lanny Johnson/Mountain Stock; p. 35 © Brooks Dodge/Mountain Stock; p. 37 ©Karl Weatherly/Mountain Stock; p. 39 © Galen Rowell/CORBIS; p. 45 © Lee Kuhn/FPG; p. 46 © John Giustina/FPG; p. 47 Kyle Krause/Mountain Stock; p. 49 © SuperStock; pp. 55, 56 © CORBIS.

Book and Series Design

Oliver H. Rosenberg